STRIPPED

*A Collection of
Inspired Writings for the
Evolving Woman*

CARA ALWILL LEYBA

STRIPPED

Cover and interior design by Ryan Leyba
Edited by Victoria Erickson

ISBN-13: 978-0692730102

For more, visit www.CaraAlwill.com
or email Info@CaraAlwill.com

For every woman on the edge of change.

A NOTE FROM THE AUTHOR

STRIPPED came to me as divine inspiration. Having written four personal development books prior, I knew I was ready to express myself and empower women in a new and artistic way, though I was uncertain of what format that would be.

Then, one day in April, like magic, poem after poem began appearing in my mind. These pieces continued to flow through me until I completed this book in August. Waterfalls of words would wake me up in the middle of the night. They consumed me during my day. I literally couldn't stop writing.

Throughout the creative process, I received what some refer to as "winks" from the universe that assured me I was doing exactly what I was meant to be doing. As a spiritual woman, I took these signs seriously and used them as inspiration to dig deeper and fully commit to this project. Suddenly, birds began appearing at my window. Hearts painted in graffiti on buildings and etched in chalk on city streets showed up in front of me multiple times per day. You'll notice in the piece "Sidewalks" I describe that experience.

You'll also notice the opening poem, "Stripped" is what inspired this entire project. This year has been a journey in committing to vulnerability, spaciousness for truth, self-acceptance, and love. Through sharing my own personal evolution, I have discovered that as women, we're all craving the opportunity to peel back the layers. So many of us are ready to remove our masks and to live authentically, without fear and without apology.

STRIPPED sets out to celebrate the power of being vulnerable and the magic that occurs when we decide to bare it all. Because life gets a hell of a lot better when we drop heaviness and take off the things we don't want to carry anymore.

With love,
Cara

She realized that
vulnerability
was easier
to wear
than vanity.
So she stripped.
Straight down to
nothing.
And set
herself free.

Wish.

Evolve.

Love.

Surrender.

Wish.

the walk

And suddenly, she began to stumble.
And her stumble soon became a crawl.
And her crawl soon became a walk.
And her walk became
a walk worth watching.
Because every time she had tripped
she got back on her feet.
She knew she could fail
and it would be okay.
Because she knew the beauty
in standing
and the grit
in fighting
was magic
worth living,
even when you fall.

UNSTOPPABLE

Think of yourself
every single day.
Think about what you need.
Who you might want to be.
What could help you be better.
Think of yourself
every singe day.
This never makes you selfish.
This makes you unstoppable.

better things

That was the thing about her.
She had this gift of seeing only possibility.
An undying reverie for better things.
Her eyes drenched in silver linings.
Living a life as though everything
was made up of magic
and every star was her own.
But the most enchanting thing about her
was that she made you feel
like you were also worthy
of that same kind of charmed universe.
Her hope was contagious.

revolution

And it was then
in that moment
that her heart filled
with all the stars
in the sky.
And it was right then
in that moment
that her soul began
its riveting
and righteous
revolution.

SHE CHOSE

She realized she had this one.
This big, bold,
and beautiful life.
And she realized
she didn't want to live it
chasing and crying
and apologizing.
Starving and fearing
and regretting.
She realized
she wanted to live it
proudly and freely
and creatively.
Lovingly and fully
and sweetly.
She realized
she could choose.
And so, she chose.

HOPE

When you let hope die,
you bury a small part of yourself.
You bury the sparks
and stars
that keep you bright
and beautiful,
open and
lit up.
So never let hope die.
Reignite it.
Set it on fire
once again.
Because we all deserve
molten-filled
worlds.

alive

You know when you can feel
that build up in your bones?
That vibration within your veins?
That humming inside of your heart?
That, my love,
is what it's all about.
That is what it feels like
to be fully,
truly,
wholly alive.
Capture those moments
and cling to them.
Scrape the ancient walls of them.
Suck them fully dry.
And let them take you home.
Every day.
In every way.

untitled

A few notes on life, and love:
You are magnificently beautiful,
even on the days when you are sad.
There are no coincidences.
Sometimes your closure
is that you may never have closure at all.
You are a fucking warrior.
Sometimes, all you need to do is laugh.
And sometimes, that is all you need.
And you always
already know the answer.

There is a world
that exists
inside you.
A starlit space
that already knows.

still

And there are still some things
that are bigger than me.
And there is humility in knowing
there are still some things
I need to grow into,
move into,
shift into.
There are still some things
I am yet
to be shaped by.

SIDEWALKS

And suddenly, everything was art.
All beautiful reminders.
Painted in chalk on city streets
and sweet sidewalks.
And every time I looked down
there was a new message waiting to be read.
Every time I looked down
I was reminded that the ground
was there to ground me.
And the floor beneath me whispered,
"I will support you, every step of your way."

bewitched

And when you actively seek magic
you will find yourself
bewitched by it daily.
Those little signs.
Those little winks.
They are not accidents,
you see.
They are here
to enchant us,
captivate us,
to ignite a starlit world
within us all.
When perhaps we have almost,
maybe,
just about
given up.

THE NEW

Treasure the mornings.
Treasure the moments
where the world comes alive.
When the sun plants a gentle
kiss on the deep horizon.
When cities awaken to buzz.
Treasure the moment
the Earth presents you with
your brand new canvas.
And know that each day
you can paint a different picture.
You can sing a new song.
You can rise with the sun
and proudly proclaim,
"Today I have a choice.
And today I'm choosing differently."

asleep/awake

Dancing on that fiery edge
of madness.
Sleeping in this warm bed
of sanity.
It's no wonder I always
kick my sheets off at night.

"Be more realistic,"
he said.
To which she replied,
"Not a chance."

MORNING WORDS

Today I choose to show up
as the best "Me" possible.
The empowered Me.
The confident Me.
The Me that handles
both anything and everything.
The Me that faces the world
with eyes of possibility,
creativity, and solution.
The Me with a heart full of hope.
The Me that expresses herself proudly.
The Me that meets others with kindness and love.
The Me that knows her strength is her best asset
because her strength paves the way for all of her choices.
The Me that knows it will be okay.
Because it always has been.

time

Because there are incredible things
and unbelievable joys
awaiting you
when you dig out
of your old despair,
when you paint over
your tired walls,
and drench yourself in hope.
So wipe off the sweat,
pick up your pen,
and whisper to your heart,
"It is time to write a new story."

Evolve.

ready

You mustn't wait
for New Year's Day.
Or Monday.
Or the first.
Or the last.
You can do it right now.
You can change right now.
You can change on an idle
Thursday afternoon at 4:45 PM
when everything inside of you
begins to stir and rattle and bang
and whisper,
"I am ready."

THE START

Embrace newness.
Immerse yourself
in the learning process.
You're only a beginner
for a small while.
Let it humble
and renew your patience
for the studious souls around you.
Everyone is trying something
for the first time.
The start only
starts once.

into gold

There is nothing
more powerful
or radical
or stunningly,
radiantly beautiful
than a woman
who chooses
to rebuild her life.
Day after day,
hour after hour,
no matter how many pieces
are hers to sweep up
or how many mistakes
she must now spin
into gold.

"You've changed."
Two of the best words
you will ever hear.

big things

Make some moves.
Not because you hate
where you are.
Make them because
you know you are capable
of being someplace
and someone
better.
Make some moves
because you are
more beautiful
and more powerful
and so much more worthy
than you give yourself credit for.
And because you deserve
big things and
big people,
and big love
always.

RISE

Don't get angry
or enraged
or insulted.
Rise above the bullshit.
Flick your light back on,
and shine it brighter than ever,
and fall so deeply in love
with your own life
that anyone who tried to wrong you
becomes a laughable, ridiculous
distant, memory.

COMING HOME

Maybe this
is what it's all for.
Maybe who you become
is who you actually
always were
before you
let the subtle whisper
of this world
become the scream.

places

If women did
half the work
on the inside
as they do
on the outside
they would be amazed
at how a life can change.
How they can attract
wildly wonderful beings
into their worlds.
How relationships can deepen.
How they can fall in love
with their own
breathing hearts.
How they can build a force field
around themselves
that will repel
anyone or anything
that does not match
their precious energy.
Looks will only take you so far.
A gorgeous soul
will take you everywhere.

please remember

Empowered women clap for one another.
Your own voice will always be louder
than an echo (be original).
You can change direction at any time.
Competing leaves you powerless.
Happiness is a choice.
You must choose it daily.
The high road never goes out of style.
Be the bigger person.
You have no idea
how stunning you really are.

THE MATCH

Never underestimate the power
of tiny steps.
There are hundreds of thousands
of mini moments
that have brought you here today
and hundreds of thousands more
that will continue to light your way.
Conversations started,
messages sent,
dreams dusted off,
invitations accepted,
flights booked,
words written.
Get out of yourself for a moment
and focus on the tiny brush strokes
that make up the painting of your life.
Realize that it is all so possible
when you think about what you can do
right here in this very moment.
Realize that you can ignite change
with nothing but a spark.
You can ignite change
simply by striking your match.

TO-DO

Tap into your creativity
each and every day.
Choose compassion over anger.
Always.
Tell someone
what they mean to you
without expectation.
Buy yourself a bouquet
of wild flowers.
Compliment a stranger.
Figure out what
sets your soul on fire.
And blow your own
damn worthy mind.

HAPPY GIRLS

Happy girls don't gossip.
Happy girls give thanks.
Happy girls become so entrenched
in their own creativity, success, and gratitude
that they have no time
for anything but love.
Love for their lives,
love for their work,
and love for the people
who remind them
of what's truly important.
The next time you find yourself
cloaked in someone else's negativity
remember that you have a choice.
Remember that you have the power
to exit any conversation
that does not make you better.
The next time someone tries
to fill your space with poison,
You can simply say,
"No thank you.
Not now.
Today and always,
 I'm choosing happiness."

dancers

It feels so good to shed the skins
of those who choose not
to evolve alongside you.
Of those who choose to remain
in just one place
with their minds cemented
in idle thinking.
I'd rather clear that space
for those who are fully alive.
For those who are spirited
and shimmering
and spinning.
For those whose souls
will twist and dance beside mine
to this never-ending song
only we can hear.

I am a melody
not meant for
everyone's ears.

POWER

A woman must understand that
power is not given to her.
It is taken.
And she must cling to it
and wrap herself up in it
and become so enveloped by it
that any other existence
feels far too small
and far too weak
for her to ever comprehend.

NOW

The most beautiful gift
you can give to yourself
is the gift of
transforming your pain.
The gift of melting
your weary anger into love.
The gift of molding
your lasting heartache into passion.
The gift of sewing
your weeping sorrow into celebration.
And the gift of realizing
that your past
does not define you.
And it never did.
And it never will.

A VOW

When we continually consume
things that are toxic,
we prolong our healing.
When we text that person,
or look at that page,
or engage
in that conversation,
or birth those thoughts,
we stifle our growth.
We send a message to ourselves
that we are not worthy
of nourishing energy,
or peace of mind.
So take a stand
for yourself
beginning today.
Choose love
over pain.
Choose peace
over chaos.
Make a vow
to choose these
every single day.
Make a vow
to begin today.

untitled

Stop feeding yourself
things that hurt.

the line

The line becomes
another world,
a larger life,
when you find the courage
to cross it.

light

Every day we have a choice.
We can live with our pain
and allow it to dress us in darkness.
Or we can step into light
transforming that hurt
into happiness.
We can remain victim
to our heartbreaks
and disappointments
and despair.
Or we can dare to smile
and dream
and fight
to fully live
bigger
and brighter
than we had ever
imagined possible.

WORTHY

You must aggressively
detox yourself
from negative thoughts,
poisonous people,
and disempowering beliefs.
You must believe
with every thread of your heart
that you are worthy.
You must make your personal evolution
a full-time job.

wish

Replace the word "selfish" with self-love.
Act in faith instead of fear.
Be inspired everyday.
Choose kindness.
Dream so big it births butterflies.
Celebrate dreams with champagne glasses.
Because you will always make it happen.
Master something you thought you couldn't do.
Be gentle with yourself.
Motivate someone who needs it.
Laugh when you want to cry,
because humor heals.
Realize you are worthy
of every single thing you want.
This is my wish for you.

the work of you

No one is coming
to save you,
to give you permission,
to choose you,
or validate you.
This has always
been your job.
You must love yourself
so fiercely
and fully
that you have no other choice
but to be strong
for yourself,
to fight for yourself,
to be yourself,
and to build yourself.

THIS WOMAN

The waves of her mind
could drown
an ocean
and the stars
in her eyes
could ignite
a whole new sky.
So watch closely.
And listen carefully.
This woman
is about to change the world.

Love.

to look at you

You must understand
in those moments
where your eyes lock
with another's,
that this is
no accident.
You must understand
that our souls pull
toward one another
to communicate
when we are too human
to find the words.
You must understand
there is a world beneath a gaze.

GLOW

Like the flicker of a flame
she will burn unending.
Her dance, unsteady at times,
but she will always
reclaim her stillness.
And once you catch her
in your sights
she will own you
with the wild way
she glows.

oceans

You are a certain type of magic
filled with stars and dreams
and one million secret thoughts.
You are a very certain type of magic
exploding with wishes
and immeasurable gifts
and oceans of hope.
You are a very certain type of magic
that has never existed before.
And will never exist
this way again.
Protect your magic
like mad,
only keeping it
for those
who also believe
in love.

ALL OF YOU

Choose someone
who will help you come undone
and stitch you whole
all at once.
Someone who will treasure
your pieces
as much as your entire picture.

symmetry

She is powerful
and vulnerable
and terrified
and always certain.
She is emblazed in her passion.
Illuminated with hope.
You will make her remember.
She will help you forget.

GUIDES

I want the wild ones.
The crazy ones.
The ones whose eyes burn
with the greatest passions.
The ones whose hearts have known
the deepest sadness.
I want the ones
who have seen
so many nights
they've learned
to light
their own torches.
I want the ones
who will teach me
how to see
and feel
what I must
while here
inside
the dark.

when we fall

And it is only
when your heart
goes blind
that you will know
the strength
of your own mad mind.

wildfire

And with certain people
you don't need words.
You have
something bigger.
Electric.
Transcending.
Bending.
Traveling like flames.
Fast and ferocious.
Gripping and violent.
Explosive and loud.
Insane and true.
And just like wildfire
it is so dangerous
yet so magnificent
to watch.

cryptic

And I'll keep tucking you away
inside these lines.
Hiding you
between my
heart and
my mind.

SMALL TALK

Magic is falling
from your mouth
and your name
drips from my fingers,
and I wonder,
how often do you think of her?
What keeps you up in the night
when your eyes are closing,
and your mind is heavy?
Are you afraid?
What fills you up with joy?
Real joy.
You know the kind-
where you are certain
you could burst right there?
Who did you truly want to be
before you told yourself
it was too late?
But instead, I'll smile,
and simply ask,
"How are you?"

everything

She is gorgeously complicated.
Sturdy yet soft.
Broken yet bound.
Joyful yet pained.
But one thing is sure,
she is all passion.
And she feels everything
deeply,
madly,
and certainly.

*You pinned my soul
against the headboard
and stole my breath
with your words.*

music

We love inside
the beat of a song.
We sing all of the words
we cannot say.

TWO SIDES

Loving you
was somewhere
between
a sweet symphony
and cruel catastrophe.
A song with
many beginnings
and a war
with no end.

old soul

He said,
"You're a dreamer, kid.
One day you'll learn."
She smiled and softly told him,
"I already have."

PAST LIFE

I think I know you from before
I think I met you somewhere else
on some fiery edge
or nostalgic ledge
elsewhere.

the edge

I don't want to sit here
and talk about tangible things.
Or be roused by facts
or goals or things for the ego.
I want to discuss magic.
I want to touch parts of you
that have been dead for years.
I want to slice you open.
I want to take you over your cliff.

OBSCURED

Let me unearth
the parts of you
that you so carefully
tuck away.
I want to get my hands dirty
from all of those words
you've been so afraid
to say.

home

She's got stars in her eyes
and dirt in her palms.
She is the kind of girl
who makes a wish
on the moon.
She is the answer
to your ongoing questions.
And also the thing
that will make you
question it all.
She is free.
She is hope.
She is home.

It is never random.
And it never was.

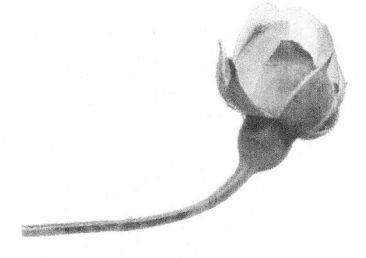

PERFECT

Don't you dare
waste another second
of precious time
believing those books
that say
you aren't enough.
Because you are perfect.
You are splendid.
You are magnificent.
And you are everything.

untitled

My eyes have poems in them.
And they will tell you
everything
my lips have yet
to say.

bones

There is a world
inside these bones.
A million wishes
and dreams unspoken
living beneath the surface
of my skin.
And I hope one day
after all this time
you will ask me
if you can come inside.

TRUE

The best kind of people
allow you the space
and the courage
to be completely
and entirely
and beautifully
yourself.

self-love

The most wonderful love
is the kind of love
where someone stops time
simply to make you happy.
The kind of love
where someone travels
to the wide ends of the Earth
just to see you smile.
The kind of love where someone
makes you a hot cup of coffee
each new morning
and makes sure
you have clean sheets
every dark night.
The kind of love
where someone tells you
that you're doing alright
even when you know you're not.
The kind of love where someone
makes you feel understood,
even when you're lost.
The most wonderful kind of love
is when someone else can give you
all of these things,
or none of them.
Because the most wonderful love
is the kind of love where
you will always be able
to give these very things
to yourself.

A BEAUTIFUL THING

Be in love at all times.
With a person.
With a place.
With a few people.
With yourself.
With life.
Just be in love with something.
Or everything.
Because a person in love
is a beautiful thing.

diamonds

You must learn
to wear your hurts
and heartbreaks
like a shimmering string
of diamonds
delicately draped around your neck
and awash with beauty so bright
one would never know
they were birthed in dirt.

THE GIFT

When I realized
I had no one
to gift me strength,
I gave it to myself.
When I realized
I had no one
to send me love,
I sent it to myself.
When I realized
I had no one to inspire me,
I inspired myself.
When I realized
I had no one
to cheer for me,
I cheered for myself.
And everything
I had once painted
as disappointment,
brought me
the beautiful discovery
of knowing everything
I had ever needed
is always within myself.
And there is no gift
more remarkable,
or empowering
or magnificent
than that.

Surrender.

STRIPPED

She realized
that vulnerability
was easier to wear
than vanity.
So she stripped.
Straight down to
nothing.
And set
herself free.

jump

Jump, my dear.
Jump into everything
and also
nothing.
Jump into the deep abyss
of bliss
that finds you
when you've finally
remembered
your
precious
self.

RAW

I'm exhausted.
Are you, too?
I'm exhausted
from all of the filters
and facades
and forced feelings
and fears
and the make-believe.
Because life is raw
and imperfect
and the real beauty
lives inside of that reality.
The real beauty
lives inside our truth.
And inside our feelings
and our fears
and sometimes
saying things like,
"I don't have this all figured out,
but I am trying."

SHAKEN

Be open to
shock treatments.
Seek them.
Invite them in.
Embrace them.
Allow them to shake
and shift
and seek you.
Then let it happen again.
And again.
And again.

all of you

Be you.
The awkward you.
The giddy you.
The strange you.
The overjoyed you.
The terrified you.
The proud you.
The hurt you.
The you that says things
and sometimes cringes.
The you that follows her heart.
The you that gets lost.
The you that tests
and tries new things.
The you that openly trusts.
Again, and again,
and again.
Just be you.
ALL of you.
Because all of you
is absolutely perfect,
and someone needs you,
exactly as you are.

*Your truth
is your
superpower.*

believe

If you believe nothing else today,
believe that there is
something else
more mystical,
more powerful,
and more lovely
than you could
ever understand.
Your only job is to let go
and trust that every beat
and every step
and every inch of your world
is lining up exactly as it should.
Let go.
And let yourself be made by magic.

SURRENDER

I want to breathe in
passion like air.
I want it to fill my lungs
with the magic
and lust
and possibility
only passion brings.
And the feeling
that is only
available to you
when you finally,
fully,
fiercely
surrender.

OPEN

Be certain of
who you are.
But open to
where you will go.
Be stone solid
in your beliefs,
and values,
and fire,
and bliss.
But do not be rock solid
with your destination.
Because life flows
and shocks
and it will rip apart
at the seams
when you finally learn
to let go.

to bleed

Vulnerability is not
simply a word.
It is a way of life.
A very certain decision.
To split yourself open
from inside out.
To peel back the layers.
To willingly bleed.
So that you can learn
to love your heart
in both the darkness,
and the light.

enough

Don't you think it's time
to celebrate the parts of ourselves
that are unpolished?
Don't you think it's time
to call bullshit on perfection?
Don't you think its time
we decide that we are enough?
Right now,
inside this exact,
imperfect,
messy moment?

WHOLE

A new idea:
Stop tucking away
all the parts of you
that don't always look
so flawless.
Stop hiding your
so-called imperfections.
Stop working overtime
to only be one single,
pretty piece of you.
Because the world needs you.
Completely.
Entirely.
Every last drop
and bit.

WHAT IF

We're always trying
to change who we are.
We strive to be
prettier, thinner,
blonder, or better.
We're always trying to
fix, and nip,
and suck and tuck.
We're always living
under the assumption
that there is an ideal woman
we should emulate;
a gold standard of beauty
to attain.
But what if our only goal
was to simply look in the mirror and say,
"There is no one else I'd rather be.
I've never met a woman better than me."

EDGES

Do not soften
your edges
for those
who are afraid
to get cut.
Remember
even a rose
can make you bleed.

brave

And suddenly one day,
all of her confidence
was replaced with questions.
Am I smart enough?
Can I really do this?
Is it even for me?
She used to feel as though
she could do anything.
So what happened?
She used to feel unstoppable.
Unbreakable.
Undeniable.
Untouchable.
And now she was reeling for answers.
She decided this
would be her assignment.
A test from the universe.
A way back to herself.
To reclaim her own life.
So she changed everything.
She changed it all.
She tried on bravery.
Because bravery was both
a beautiful outfit
and a book of matches
and she used it
to burn down the whole fucking house.
And she passed that test.
She passed with flying colors.
And built a brand new world.

FLY

Do not allow your fear
to become flames.
Do not allow your worry
to become wildfire.
There is simply too much
awaiting you
when you drop heaviness
and allow faith to fly.

made from stars

Beautiful girl,
you are made of stardust
and white hot love
and symphonies
and one thousand mysteries.
Beautiful girl,
why won't you finally believe
that you are magic?

PRICELESS

Know your worth.
Every last cent.
Every sweet gift.
Know your worth.
And realize that nobody
will ever possess the power
to duplicate your beauty,
imitate your brilliance,
or replicate your radiance.
Know your worth.
Because your voice
will always be louder
than an echo.

INTUITION

Learn to value solitude.
Learn to gamble on your gut,
and let it guide you.
You already have everything you need.
Nobody else can direct your next step
or illuminate your way.
Learn to love the universe inside of you.
It will never, ever
lead you astray.

*It is your duty
to listen to the world
that is calling
your name.*

moments

Sometimes
there will be these very tiny moments
where you may find yourself
melting into someone's laughter
or admiring the clouds
or the beauty of a bird
or the way the wind
can shake and shift
the petal of a plant.
And in these tiny moments
when you sink more in love
with everything
and everyone
you realize
these moments
are not tiny
at all.

PATIENT

When you're in divine flow
words and movement
should feel effortless.
Struggle occurs when we
push against the plan
the universe has for us.
Embrace every moment.
Be completely present.
Allow yourself
the space to bloom.
Remain in tune
with your highest purpose.
And most importantly,
be still within those moments
when you want to fight.
Those are the ones
that will teach you the most.

BURN

I hope you set
your wild heart on fire.
I hope you find freedom
inside of those
wretched,
white hot,
seething,
smoldering,
flames.

a woman's truth

Do your thing.
Do it without fear
or apology.
Infuse your essence
into everything.
No one can deny
the unvarnished truth
of a woman.

not for you

It is not your responsibility
to win over others
who have already made judgments
of your character.
It is not your responsibility
to apologize for someone else's
interpretation of your intention.
It is not your responsibility
to teach someone
the language of your heart.

HER CHOICE

After a while
you learn your choices
are not wrong, nor right.
They are simply your choices.
Decisions guided from the inside.
Illuminated on the outside.
The heart always knows
what to decide.
And every one of them is yours.
And every one of them is true.

vulnerable

It was like I had
ripped a seam.
And instead of frantically
trying to sew it back up
I pulled at the threads
more and more
and more,
until they
unraveled completely
and then transformed
into the most beautiful
tapestry I'd ever worn.

YOU ARE HER

We spend so much time
looking outside ourselves
for the answers,
the happiness,
the permission.
Why can't we believe
that it is all inside?
What will it take to realize
that the woman
you spend so much energy
trying to become
is the woman
you already are?

*Burn down
your walls.
It is
breathtaking
inside.*

BY THE SAME AUTHOR

Girl Code: Unlocking the Secrets to Success, Sanity, and Happiness for the Female Entrepreneur

Fearless & Fabulous: 10 Powerful Strategies for Getting Anything You Want in Life

The Champagne Diet: Eat, Drink, and Celebrate Your Way to a Healthy Mind and Body

Sparkle: The Girl's Guide to Living a Deliciously Dazzling, Wildly Effervescent, Kick-Ass Life

MEET THE AUTHOR
cara alwill leyba

As a best selling author, master life coach and creator of The Champagne Diet brand, Cara Alwill Leyba empowers women to live their most effervescent lives, celebrate themselves every day, and make their happiness a priority. She is passionate about helping women style their minds and design their lives in a chic and stylish way. Her glamorous approach to self-help has attracted thousands of women to read her books and blog, and attend her workshops and events.

Cara has previously self-published four books which have all reached #1 on various best seller categories on Amazon including Self-Help, Self-Esteem, Motivation, and Women in Business, and have gained massive popularity around the world.

Cara's work has been featured in *Glamour, Shape, Vibe, Huffington Post, PopSugar, Cosmopolitan,* and *Marie Claire,* to name a few. She has been a speaker at the American Chamber of Commerce in Tokyo where she educated its members about the power of personal branding. In 2015, Cara was named one of *YFS Magazine*'s "Top 10 Women Entrepreneurs That Will Inspire You."

For more about Cara, please visit www.CaraAlwill.com

Follow Cara on Instagram for daily inspiration
@TheChampagneDiet